Fact Finders®

The
Solar System
and Beyond

Stars

by Kristine Carlson Asselin

Consultant:
Dániel Apai, PhD
Space Telescope Science Institute
Baltimore, Maryland

CAPSTONE PRESS
a capstone imprint

Fact Finders are published by Capstone Press,
151 Good Counsel Drive, P.O. Box 669, Mankato, Minnesota 56002.
www.capstonepub.com

Books published by Capstone Press are manufactured with paper
containing at least 10 percent post-consumer waste.

Library of Congress Cataloging-in-Publication Data
Asselin, Kristine Carlson.
Stars / by Kristine Carlson Asselin.
p. cm.—(Fact finders. The solar system and beyond)
Includes bibliographical references and index.
Summary: "Describes stars, including births and deaths, types of stars, and
constellations"—Provided by publisher.
ISBN 978-1-4296-5398-5 (library binding)
ISBN 978-1-4296-6243-7 (paperback)
1. Stars—Juvenile literature. I. Title. II. Series.
QB801.7.A89 2011
523.8—dc22   2010026025

Editorial Credits
Jennifer Besel, editor; Heidi Thompson, designer; Eric Manske, production specialist

Photo Credits
Alamy: Galaxy Picture Library, 21, PHOTOTAKE Inc., 20; iStockphoto/essxboy, 26; NASA and The
Hubble Heritage Team (STScl/AURA), 9; NASA, ESA, and Martino Romaniello (European Southern
Observatory, Germany), 23; NASA, ESA, The Hubble Key Project Team, and The High-Z Supernova
Search Team, 11; NASA, ESA, The Hubble SM4 ERO Team, 14–15; NASA/JPL-Caltech/T. Megeath
(University of Toledo) & M. Robberto (STScl), 7; Peter Arnold: Biosphoto/Pacelli Laurent, 25; Photo
Researchers, Inc: Baback Tafreshi, 29, Gerard Lodriguss, 27, John Chumack, 3, 17, Mark Garlick, 19;
Shutterstock: Konstantin Mironov, 5, Primož Cigler, cover, 1; SOHO, 13

Artistic Effects
iStockphoto: appleuzr, Dar Yang Yan, Nickilford

Printed in the United States of America in Stevens Point, Wisconsin.
092010   005934WZS11

Table of Contents

Chapter 1

Twinkling Stars

Since the dawn of humankind, people have observed patterns of stars moving in the sky. For ancient people, the stars were as familiar as their own families. In fact, they thought the twinkling stars were gods living in the heavens.

Today we know the stars aren't gods. They are fiery balls of gas. And our Sun is just one of billions of stars in the universe.

On a dark night, you can see about 3,000 stars without a telescope. But there are many, many others you can't see. More than 100 billion stars shine in our Milky Way **galaxy** alone. To get an idea of that number, imagine a football field covered with a layer of baseballs. Now keep adding layers of balls 12 miles (19 kilometers) into the sky. And that's just the Milky Way. There are billions of galaxies each with hundreds of billions of stars.

galaxy: a large group of stars and planets

FACT: Stars don't twinkle in space. Earth's atmosphere breaks up starlight, making the stars seem to glow and fade.

the Milky Way as seen from Earth

Birth of a Star

Stars are born inside spinning molecular clouds. Gravity causes a cloud to pull in on itself and spin faster. Think of how a figure skater spins faster by pulling her arms closer to her body. The same is true as the cloud pulls in. As the cloud collapses, a huge mass builds up in its core. Hydrogen atoms crash and join together in the center of the forming star. This process, called nuclear fusion, causes the star to get incredibly hot. The hotter it gets, the more the hydrogen atoms stick and the brighter the forming star shines.

Some gases and dust pieces in the cloud spin so fast they cannot land on the star. The gas and dust creates a disk around the forming star. Planets will form out of this disk. The energy released during a star's birth bathes the surrounding space in heat and light.

molecular cloud: a giant cloud made mostly of hydrogen atoms bound together

gravity: a force that pulls objects together

image of the Orion Nebula taken by the Hubble Space Telescope

FACT: Thousands of stars have been born in the Orion Nebula, an area in a molecular cloud. In fact, new stars are forming right now!

Aging Stars

Stars live for billions of years. During their lifetimes, they go through different phases. Scientists call new stars young stellar objects. New stars are hard to see because the clouds that formed them also block them from view. The light from these young stars varies, growing and dimming.

Over millions of years, the young stars become less variable. They shine and keep a constant temperature. These adult stars are called main sequence stars. They shine brightly thanks to nuclear fusion.

Stars remain in the main sequence phase for billions of years. But eventually each star burns away the hydrogen in its core and starts to die. Gravity pulls matter down on the core. The pressure causes nuclear fusion to start in layers around the core. This extra energy causes the star to expand and get brighter. As it expands, its outer layers cool. The star becomes redder and is called a red giant.

a supergiant star

a cluster of young, hot stars

When stars run out of nuclear fuel, most become white dwarfs. A white dwarf is similar to a hot ember left after a fire has burned out. It's not burning, but it's still very hot at about 180,000 degrees Fahrenheit (100,000 degrees Celsius). Eventually, the white dwarf cools and fades away.

Spectacular Deaths

Stars that have high **mass** die a more spectacular death. When a high-mass star burns out of the main sequence phase, it becomes a red supergiant. Then, instead of cooling to a white dwarf, gravity causes the star's core to collapse. The crushing of the core eventually sends a shockwave through the star, blowing it apart. Called a supernova, this explosion produces a fireball millions of times brighter than the Sun.

When the explosion is over, all that's left is a small core. If the core has very little mass, it becomes a spinning, dark neutron star. But if the core is still as massive as three or more Suns, gravity once again takes over. The core collapses into itself very tightly. The star becomes a black hole. A black hole is an object with such strong gravity that even light cannot escape from it.

mass: the amount of material in an object

image of a supernova in Galaxy NCG 4526 taken by the Hubble Space Telescope

Chapter 2

Star Features

Billions of stars light up outer space. And just like people, those stars are all different ages. Most stars are in the main sequence phase of their life cycle. In this phase, the stars are called dwarfs. Most stars stay in this stage for 10 billion to 1,000 billion years. Right now our Sun is a dwarf star.

When stars begin to die, their outer layers expand. Stars in this phase are called giants or supergiants. Supergiants, the biggest stars, can have a **radius** 1,000 times greater than the Sun.

Many of the oldest stars are white dwarfs. All that's left of these stars is a small, hot, glowing core.

Stars live so long that a scientist can't watch one go from birth to death. So scientists figure out what phase a star is in by studying features such as color, temperature, size, and brightness.

radius: a straight line drawn from the center of a circle to its outer edge

The Sun is closer to Earth than any other star. It's the only star scientists have close-up images of.

Color and Temperature

A star's color tells scientists how hot its surface is. Star colors range from red to blue. It might seem a little backward, but red stars are actually the coolest. Blue stars have the hottest surface temperatures.

Scientists group stars based on their surface temperatures. Red stars are called M-type stars. Yellow stars, like our Sun, are G-type stars.

Star Type	Color	Surface Temperature in Degrees Fahrenheit	Surface Temperature in Degrees Celsius
O	blue	more than 54,000	more than 30,000
B	blue-white	18,000–54,000	10,000–30,000
A	white	13,000–18,000	7,300–10,000
F	white-yellow	10,800–13,000	6,000–7,300
G	yellow	8,900–10,800	4,900–6,000
K	orange	6,500–8,900	3,600–4,900
M	red	less than 6,500	less than 3,600

FACT: Scientists use a fun saying to remember the star types, "Oh Be A Fine Girl, Kiss Me."

a small part of the Omega Centauri star cluster in the Milky Way, showing stars of many types

Brightness

Scientists gather clues about stars based on their brightness or **apparent magnitude**. Each star is compared to the star Vega. Vega has an apparent magnitude of almost 0. Stars brighter than Vega get a negative number as their magnitude. Stars dimmer than Vega have positive numbers. Polaris, the North Star, has a magnitude of 2.0. The Sun has a magnitude of -26.7.

Two things affect the apparent magnitude of a star. The first is the actual amount of light the star creates. The second is the distance from Earth to the star. A dim star looks very bright when it's close to our planet. But some very bright stars look dim because they are far away. Take the stars Sirius and Canopus, for example. Sirius is 8.6 **light-years** from Earth and has an apparent magnitude of about -1.5. Canopus looks dimmer from Earth, with a magnitude of -0.7. But Canopus is 312 light-years away.

apparent magnitude: a measure of how bright a star looks from Earth

light-year: a unit used to measure distance in space; 1 light-year equals about 6 trillion miles (9.5 trillion kilometers)

Brightest Stars

Star	Apparent Magnitude	Distance from Earth
Sun	-26.7	93 million miles (150 million kilometers)
Sirius	-1.46	8.6 light-years
Canopus	-0.72	312 light-years
Alpha Centauri	-0.29	4.4 light-years
Arcturus	-0.04	37 light-years
Vega	+0.03	25 light-years

Vega

FACT: If you could study Canopus and the Sun side by side, Canopus would shine about 13,300 times brighter than our Sun.

Chapter 3

Star Hopping

The Sun is the only star scientists can study at relatively close range. Our star is about 93 million miles (150 million km) away from Earth. By studying the Sun, astronomers are able to learn a lot about all stars.

The Sun is a medium-sized, yellow, main sequence star in the Milky Way galaxy. It was born about 4.6 billion years ago. The Sun's gravity keeps everything in our solar system revolving around it.

Compared to other stars, our Sun's really not an extraordinary star. Many bigger, brighter stars have solar systems spinning around them. But the Sun is special for one reason. It supports life on Earth.

Comparing Star Sizes

Rigel

Antares

Sirius A

Sun

Sirius

The brightest star in the night sky is Sirius. It is about twice the size of the Sun. It is also much hotter, which is why it appears to shine so brightly. Sirius is one of our closest star neighbors. You can easily see it on a clear night without a telescope. This star has a distinct blue color. Scientists call it an A-type star.

Polaris, the North Star

Polaris

Polaris is also known as the North Star. This star seems to stay still in the sky while everything else spins around it. In the Northern Hemisphere, it is visible year-round, always pointing the way north. Polaris is 430 light-years away. The star is a type F supergiant star. It is 2,500 times brighter than our Sun.

Star Systems

Stars that form from the same cloud are often held close together by gravity. These star clusters can include hundreds or millions of stars.

While our Sun is a solo star, about 75 percent of all stars are part of groups called binary systems. In these systems multiple stars **orbit** one another. But unless you look at them with a telescope, they look like a single star.

The star closest to our Sun is called Proxima Centauri. This star is part of a group of three stars called the Alpha Centauri system. This system is about four light-years from Earth.

In 1862, astronomer Alvan Clark discovered that Sirius is also a binary star. Its companion star, Sirius B, was the first white dwarf ever discovered.

orbit: the path an object follows as it goes around a star

a cluster of stars in the Large Magellanic Cloud that scientists believe is 50 million years old

Chapter 4

Pictures in the Sky

Ancient astronomers studied the stars as a way to understand their world. To keep the stars organized, they divided the sky into patterns called constellations. They named these constellations after gods and animals. Today scientists recognize 88 constellations.

The constellations we see today have not changed much since prehistoric times. The stars are so far away, any movement they have made seems minor. But the stars do seem to move together through the sky each night. This movement happens because Earth is spinning around on its **axis**.

The positions of the stars also change as the Earth orbits the Sun. As the Earth moves around the Sun, our view of other stars changes. That's why some constellations can be seen in some seasons and not in others.

axis: an imaginary line that runs through the middle of a planet

Orion

One of the best-known constellations is Orion. Also known as the Hunter, this constellation is named for the son of Poseidon in Greek mythology.

The constellation includes two spectacular stars. Betelgeuse (BEET-el-joose) is one of the largest stars scientists have found. This red supergiant shines with the light of more than 50,000 Suns.

Rigel is a blue supergiant star in the Orion constellation. Rigel means "foot" in Arabic. This star marks one of the Hunter's feet.

Orion

Betelgeuse α

Bellatrix

λ

μ

φ1

φ2

δ

ε

η

ζ

Neb. Tête de Cheval'

M42-43

β

Rigel

χ

Saiph

π4

π5

π6

Ursa Major

Ursa Major, or the Great Bear, is the third largest constellation. This constellation features one of the most famous star patterns in the sky—the Big Dipper. The Big Dipper is not an official constellation. The familiar bowl and handle are actually the back end and tail of the Great Bear.

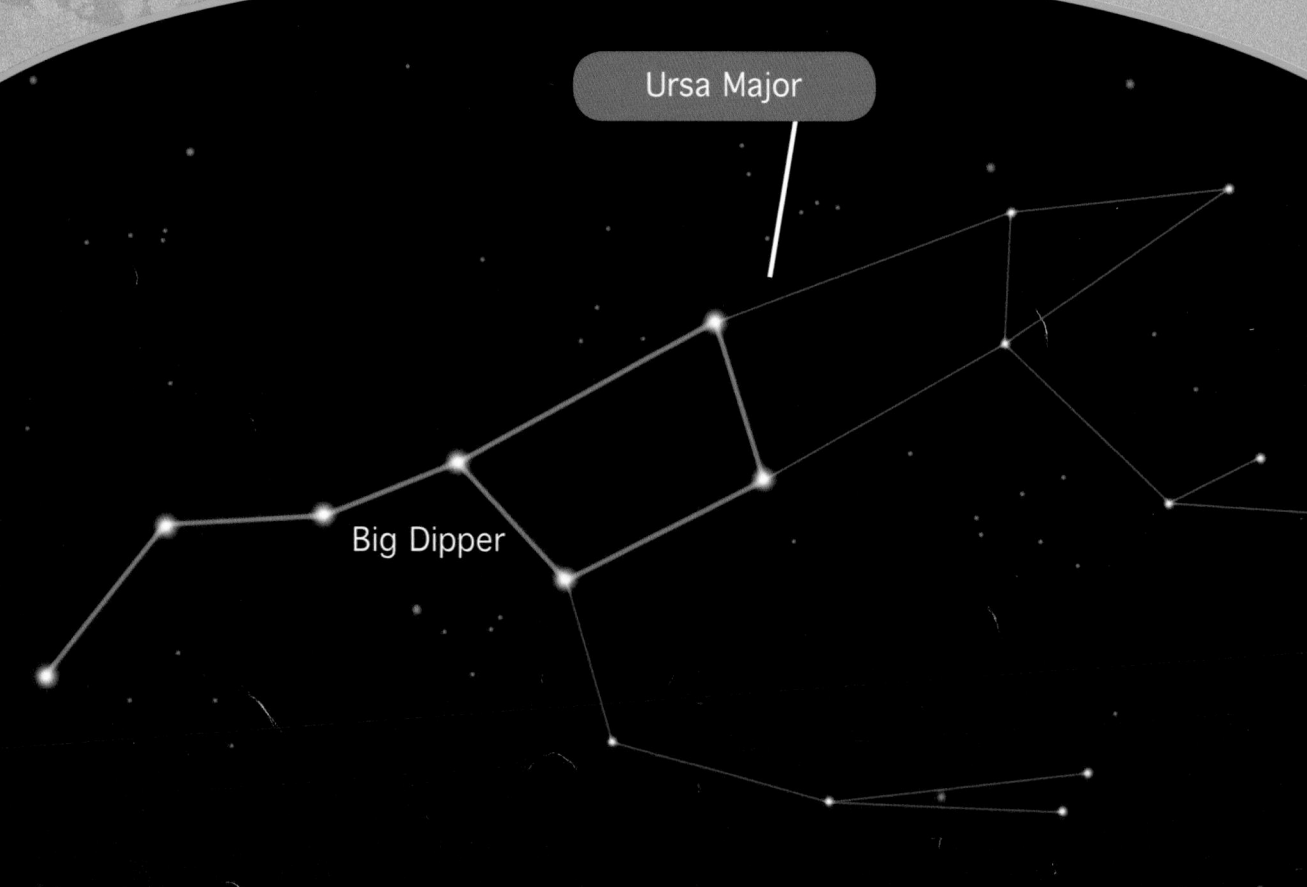

Ursa Major

Big Dipper

Ursa Minor

Little Dipper

Polaris

The two stars on the end
of the Big Dipper's bowl point
to Polaris, the North Star.

Big Dipper

Dubhe

Merak

Ursa Minor

Ursa Minor, or the Lesser Bear, is also a
famous constellation. This constellation features
the Little Dipper. The star at the very tip of the
dipper's handle is the famous North Star—Polaris.
The handle of the Little Dipper is also the Lesser
Bear's tail. The Dipper's cup is the Bear's side.

Chapter 5

Shining Neighbors

People have been stargazing as long as we have walked on the planet. Ancient humans tracked the seasons by watching the constellations move across the sky. They used the stars as guides when they traveled. They even imagined gods and heroes fighting battles in the skies.

Humans haven't changed all that much. We know stars and constellations aren't gods. But we still want to know what's out there. The stars are beautiful nightly reminders of Earth's small place in the universe. They are our stellar neighbors, shining from trillions of miles away.

FACT: The light we see from stars is a thing from the past. For example, Betelgeuse is 430 light-years away. We see the star as it was in the year 1600—about the time the Pilgrims landed in North America!

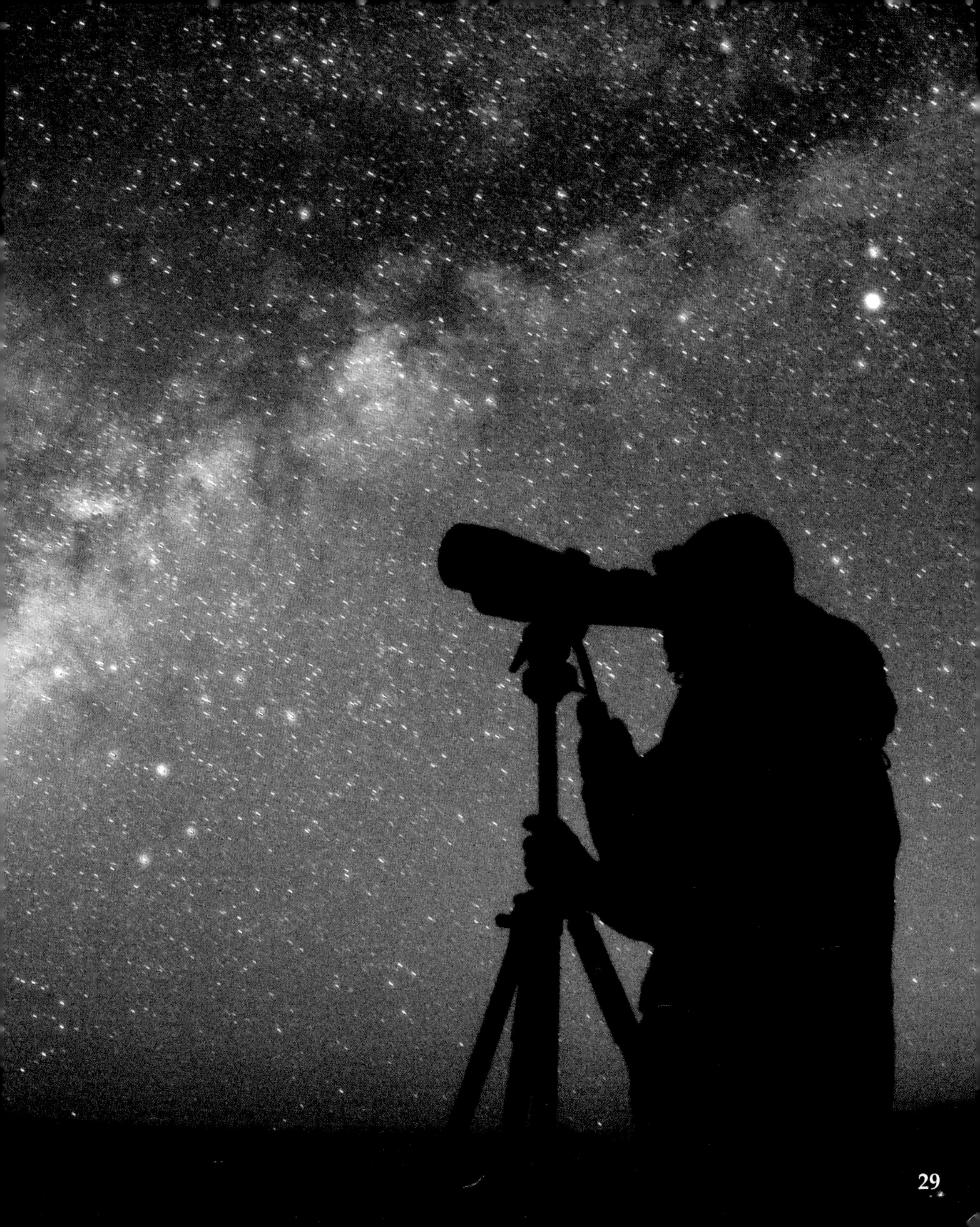

Glossary

apparent magnitude (uh-PAIR-uhnt MAG-nuh-tood)—a measure of how bright a star looks from Earth

axis (AK-sis)—an imaginary line that runs through the middle of a dwarf planet, moon, or planet; a dwarf planet, moon, or planet spins on its axis

core (KOR)—the inner part of a star, planet, or dwarf planet

galaxy (GAL-uhk-see)—a large group of stars and planets

gravity (GRAV-uh-tee)—a force that pulls objects together; gravity increases as the mass of objects increases or as objects get closer

light-year (LITE-yihr)—a unit for measuring distance in space; a light-year is the distance that light travels in one year

mass (MASS)—the amount of material in an object

molecular cloud (muh-LEK-yuh-lur KLOUD)—a cloud trillions of miles across made mostly of hydrogen atoms bound together; new stars form deep within the cores of molecular clouds

orbit (OR-bit)—the path an object follows as it goes around a dwarf planet, planet, or star

radius (RAY-dee-uhss)—a straight line segment drawn from the center of a circle to its outer edge

Read More

Asselin, Kristine Carlson. *Our Sun*. The Solar System and Beyond. Mankato, Minn.: Capstone Press, 2011.

Kim, F. S. *Constellations*. A True Book. New York.: Children's Press, 2010.

Mack, Gail. *The Stars*. Space! Tarrytown, N.Y.: Marshall Cavendish Benchmark, 2010.

Scott, Elaine. *Space, Stars, and the Beginning of Time: What the Hubble Telescope Saw*. Boston, N.Y.: Clarion Books, 2011.

Internet Sites

FactHound offers a safe, fun way to find Internet sites related to this book. All of the sites on FactHound have been researched by our staff.

Here's all you do:

Visit *www.facthound.com*

Type in this code: 9781429653985

 Check out projects, games and lots more at
www.capstonekids.com

Index